# My Friend's Robot Girlfriend
# and
# Other Humorous Verses

## Kevin Morris

# Contents

# Acknowledgements

I would like to thank the following:

Dave Higgins for proof reading and formatting my manuscript (any remaining errors are entirely my own).

And Shanelle Webb, Jeff Grant, and Ophelia Nelly May Humphreys-Elvis who all helped by encouraging me to produce this collection, and by commenting on my work.

## A Beautiful Young Lady Named White

A beautiful young lady named White
Brought delight to me last night.
In a backstreet hotel
That I know well,
We composed poetry all last night.

## A Man Who Is a Terrible Sinner

A man who is a terrible sinner
Came round to mine for his dinner.
His name being Paul,
He ate it all.
As for me? I grew much thinner!

## A Most Enterprising Young Lady Named Maddy

A most enterprising young lady named Maddy
Is looking for a rich sugar daddy.
When I had money
I was her honey.
But now I've been dumped by Maddy...

## I Awoke to a Very Loud Knocking

I awoke to a very loud knocking,
In bed with the beautiful Miss Hocking.
She said, "I can not pretend
That I don't have a boyfriend!"
I said, "Is that him knocking, Hocking?"

# I Know a Young Lady Named Coral

I know a young lady named Coral
Who is stern and ever so moral.
The good vicar Spink
Gave me a wink.
I think he knows more about Coral...

## I Know a Young Lady Named Lou

I know a young lady named Lou
Who is known for losing her shoe.
My friend Miss Hocking
Loses many a stocking
When she visits me along with Lou...

## I Met a Young Lady Named Ling

I met a young lady named Ling
And enjoyed a bit of a fling.
All went real well,
Then, sad to tell,
Ling suggested I buy her a ring...!

## I Met a Young Lady Named Marge

I met a young lady named Marge
Who posts lots of ads for massage.
But when I got there,
A police constable called Claire
Charged me and Marge on a barge!

## I Met a Young Lady Named Steed

I met a young lady named Steed
Who said, "I have a great need!"
Dear reader, I must confess,
She was wearing no dress
Which distracted my steed from his feed!

## I Met a Young Nun in December

I met a young nun in December
Who gave me a night to remember.
A very old monk
Snored in his bunk,
While that nun sang hymns in December!

# I Once Had a Lover Named Glover

I once had a lover named Glover
Who said she would have no other.
But I caught her with Moriah
And the entire male voice choir...
And a vicar who knows my mother!

## I Once Met a Girl with a Lettuce

I once met a girl with a lettuce
Who spoke to me of her peculiar fetish.
Some girls they love whipped cream
But to me it does seem
That you can't beat a girl's fetish lettuce!

# I Once Met a Very Eminent Professor

I once met a very eminent professor
Who lived in a large Welsh dresser.
When I asked him why
He heaved a great sigh
And said, "You're not my Father Confessor!"

## Keith the Thief

There was a young man named Keith
Who was known as a prodigious thief;
Until Miss Rose and Miss Hocking
Tied him up with their stockings,
Which delighted that young man named Keith!

# Lin Who Was Fond of Very Fine Gin

I knew an old lady named Lin
Who was fond of very fine gin.
I am pleased to say
That she has passed away
And left me some very fine gin...!

## Ling Who Likes to Dance and Sing

A young lady named Ling
Likes to dance and sing.
In the depths of the dark,
The dogs howl and bark
And neighbours throw things at Ling!

## My Friend the Late Lord Kettle

My great friend the late Lord Kettle
Said, "I am quite unable to settle."
Then he made some tea,
Which he shared with me,
In a place that's known as Settle.

## Maude

I know a young lady named Maude
Who makes love on an ironing board.
Her husband Ted
Prefers the bed.
But I'm fond of Maude's ironing board...

## Miss Glover's Lover

I met a young lady named Glover
Who asked could she be my lover.
She said, just for me,
She'd throw in Miss Leigh,
Which delighted that young lady's dear mother!

## Miss Hall's Crystal Ball

I met a young lady named Hall
Who said, "gaze into my crystal ball!"
When I looked therein
I saw great sin,
So went home with gorgeous Miss Hall!

## Miss Ria's New Year

There was a young lady named Ria
Who, it being a brand new year,
Drank a whole bottle of wine;
Which was more or less fine
But then she turned to strong beer...!

## Miss Rose and My Bedclothes

When I found naughty Miss Rose
Sleeping nude under my new bedclothes,
I said, "My dear,
The bishop draws near;
We'd better stay under these bedclothes!"

## Murry's Hot Curry

There was a young man named Murry
Who fell into a very hot curry.
When they said, "Are you okay?"
He said, "It's a cold day!
But I'm hot here in this curry!"

## Dirty Weekend

When a close friend of my girlfriend
Invited us to spend a dirty weekend,
We entered the deep wood
And fell in the mud!
But let's return to our dirty weekend...!

## Miss Khan's Barn

I know a young lady named Khan
Who invites me into her old barn.
In the new stable,
Miss Mabel is able,
While Khan works hard in that barn.

## My Friend's Robot Girlfriend

I am very surprised that my friend
Has gone and bought a robot girlfriend.
She is extremely pretty
And really quite witty;
So she is quite unlike my friend!

## My Lady of Ill Repute

I met a lady of ill repute
Who played all night on my flute.
We had a bit to drink,
But it's not what you think...
As that flute I bought in Beirut!

## Halloween Train Journey

I travelled on a train to Bath
Which was manned by a skeleton staff.
It was on the night of Halloween
And all the passengers did loudly scream.
But the skeletons got us to Bath!

## Party Time

A young lady who is really arty
Is a member of the Labour Party.
Her Conservative old lover
Has a Communist brother
Who likes to dress as a smarty!

## Party Girl

A poet rhymes
Of party time.
Hyped at night
On dusty lines
And cigarettes,
She feels unreal
But never forgets
Her lines.

## Procrastination

When a young lady named Kate
Said, "Kevin, you really do procrastinate!"
I said, "I beg your pardon!
But I am doing this garden!
But perhaps the garden can wait…"

## Rose Who is Forever Crossing Her Toes

I know a young lady named Rose
Who is known for crossing her toes.
When I say to her, "Honey,
Why do you walk so funny?"
She says, "I'm forever crossing my toes!"

# Sherry

A man whose name is Terry
Is extremely fond of his Sherry.
As for me,
I like tea
And sometimes I enjoy Miss Sherry...

## Squire Pleasant

My uncle, the good-natured Squire Pleasant,
Invited me to go and shoot peasant.
I went with my spouse
And found peasants and grouse...
And the police who arrested Squire Pleasant!

# There Once Was a Very Clever Goose

There once was a very clever goose
Who, at Christmas, decided to break loose.
As he flew from the farmyard
He said, "This life is hard:
As the farmer, he has no goose!"

## The Drunk Monk

I've just met a very old monk
Who stood in the pub getting drunk.
He said, "Sweet barmaid Claire
Let us have an affair!"
Have you seen a black-eyed monk...?

# Discretion

I met a young lady with petite feet
Who said, "Please promise you will be discreet."
I went back with Grace
To her sweet little place.
She lives at 7 Such and Such Street...

## The Old Rake Lake

I know an old man named Lake
Who is known as a terrible rake.
He spends his days sinning
With all kinds of women.
How I envy that old rake Lake...!

# The Poetic Old Goat

I know a most poetic old goat
Who composes poetry whilst in a moat.
A young lady named Gwen
Is due here at 10.
She calls me her poetic old goat...!

## The Poisoned Pen

When a young lady named Henrietta
Sent me a poisoned pen letter,
I said to Miss Gale,
"Hasn't she heard of email?
It's much quicker than a letter!"

# The Sad Demise of a Clown

When a clown whose name was Moat
Sang as he sank in a boat,
His friend Guy
Began to cry
At the loss of his new boat...

## The Vicar's Bed

When a naughty young lady named White
Climbed into the vicar's bed last night,
His sweet mistress Claire
Said to Miss Flair,
"Was it you who invited Miss White?"

# Prufrock's Lost Sock

There once was a man named Prufrock
Who became known for losing a sock.
He dreamed of a mermaid
(Who was far from staid)
So I guess she kept his sock!

## There Once Was a Man with an Easel

There once was a man with an easel
Who made friends with a wise old weasel.
He painted great lakes
And big juicy steaks,
While the man he would hold that easel.

## The Wicked Old Cat

There once was a most wicked old cat
Who ate many a fine gentleman's top hat.
He lived in a house
With a very bad mouse
And a rat who was known as Matt!

## Police Constable Rose

There once was a police constable named Rose
Who was well known for wearing plain clothes.
A man called Matt
Wore only his hat
And got arrested by Rose in plain clothes...!

# The Short Sighted Hairdresser

There once was a short-sighted hairdresser
Who confessed to the great Father Confessor.
He said to her, "Bess,
It is right to confess.
But you are addressing my Welsh dresser!"

## There Once Was an Angel Named Lin

There once was an angel named Lin
Who wished to dance on a pin.
But a wicked old mortal
Tempted her through his portal,
Which led to great wickedness and sin!

## There Was a Young Lady Named Flow

There was a young lady named Flow
Who lived in a fine old bureau.
When they said, "What an antique!"
She would awake from her sleep
And say, "No, I'm young Miss Flow!"

# Bert Who Liked to Dress in a Skirt

There was a young man named Bert
Who liked to dress in a skirt.
A girl called Lou
Lent him one shoe
So he hopped along in that skirt!

## Giles Who Dressed in Tiles

There was a young man named Giles
Who walked around wearing nothing but tiles.
When he fell with a crash,
All the tiles they went smash
And the girls wore very big smiles…!

## There Was a Young Man of Boulder

There was a young man of Boulder
Who carried a chip on his shoulder.
They said to him, "Matt,
You need to lose that!
Along with that fish on your shoulder!"

# When a Careless Young Person Named Mole

When a careless young person named Mole
Slipped and fell into an open manhole,
A rat called Matt
Ate his new hat;
And the Devil, he swallowed Mole's soul!

## When a Naughty Young Lady Named Kate

When a naughty young lady named Kate
Said, "I'll have you on a plate!"
I said to Mabel,
"Quick! Clear the table!
Or Kate she will break my plate!"

# When a Vicious Young Man of Bristol

When a vicious young man of Bristol
Threatened me with his rapier and pistol,
A girl named Lake
Distracted him with cake
And I whacked him with Miss Crystal!

# When a Young Lady in a Hurry

When a young lady in a hurry
Fell into a hot plate of curry,
A diner from Madras
Raised his wine glass
And toasted that girl in his curry!

## When a Young Lady Known as Prism

When a young lady known as Prism
Said, "The sun he has just risen"
And they said, "Claire!
Beware of that bear!"
She said, "My name it is Prism!"

## When a Young Lady Reading a Thriller

When a young lady reading a thriller
Accused me of being a serial killer,
I said, "Miss Hocking!
Your suggestion is shocking!
But I admit to writing that thriller!"

## When a Young Lady Smoking a Cigar

When a young lady smoking a cigar
Said, "Has anyone seen my new bra?"
An ageing rake known as Morris
Passed her The Odes of Horace...
But he kept that young lady's bra!

## When a Young Lady Washing the Dishes

When a young lady washing the dishes
Said, "have you seen my pet fishes?"
I said to her, "Claire,
You should take more care!
You're washing those fishes with the dishes!"

## When a Young Lady Wearing a Hat

When a young lady wearing a hat
Said, "Tell me, do you fancy that?"
I said, "Miss Coral,
I'm far too moral;
But I really do like that hat!"

## When a Young Lady Who is Divine

When a young lady who is divine
Came round to mine with some wine,
It ended in the lake
With a large cream cake
And the vicar at just gone 9...!

## When a Young Lady Who is Exotic

When a young lady who is exotic
Suggested that we do something very erotic,
I said to her, "Lou,
I would really love to,
But my wife she is very despotic!"

## When a Young Man Eating a Trifle

When a young man eating a trifle
Got shot by an old-fashioned rifle,
A policeman named Ted
Said, "He is dead!
Which is serious, and no mere trifle!"

# When an Elderly Gentleman Named Nool

When an elderly gentleman named Nool
Fell from a high bar stool,
A doctor called Ted
Said, "He's stone dead!"
And I quickly grabbed that stool!

## Naughty Miss Mabel

When I found naughty Miss Mabel
Making love on my dining table,
I said to Ted,
"What about my bed?"
He said, "I prefer Miss Mabel…!"

# The Easter Bunny

When I met with the Easter Bunny
She called me 'sweet' and 'her honey'.
She came back to mine
And, after kisses and wine,
That bunny she left with my money...!

## The Ghost of Edgar Alan Poe

When the ghost of Edgar Alan Poe
Appeared to a young lady named Flow,
She said to him, "Sir,
My name it is Claire."
Why she lied, I really don't know!

# I Know a Young Lady of Pleasure

I know a young lady of pleasure
Who says her name it is Heather.
I was warned by mum
To avoid the hot sun;
But she didn't say anything about Heather…!

## Alibi

A man whose name was Wood
Said my poetry was no good.
In the forest dark
His end was stark.
But my alibi it was good...

# First Class

As I boarded a first class carriage
I met a young lady from Harwich.
When she suggested an affair,
I said to her, "Claire!
Not here in this first class carriage!"

## As I Walked Home One Dark Halloween

As I walked home one dark Halloween
I heard a most ear-piercing scream.
I said to Miss Black,
"We must not look back!"
But she'd vanished with a piercing scream!

## Being Known

As I strolled through the great Crystal Palace
I met with a young lady named Alice.
When she gave me a wink
And said, "Me and Miss Spink?"
I said, "I'm known here in Crystal Palace...!"

## Blackpool Sand

I once had a one-night stand
With a young lady on Blackpool sand.
When the tide came in,
I wept for my sin
And abandoned that girl on the sand...!

## I Awoke with a Gorgeous Lap Dancer

I awoke with a gorgeous lap-dancer
Who said, "Sir, you are a chancer!"
I said, "Dear Miss Follit,
Have you seen my wallet?"
She said, "Sir, I'm also a chancer!"

## Claire Who Got Eaten by a Large Brown Bear

When a young lady whose name was Claire
Got eaten by a rather large brown bear,
Her poor boyfriend Guy
Said, with a sigh,
"I guess that's the end of our affair..."

# Doppelganger

There is a young lady named White
Who is known as The Gentlemen's Delight.
She works in a club
With that gorgeous Miss Grub
And my doppelganger was there last night...!

## Elane Who Liked to Dance in the Rain

There was a young lady named Elane
Who liked to dance in the rain.
When the weather was dry,
She would weep and sigh;
Then sing, which brought on the rain!

# Gale Who Swung from the Curtain Rail

There was a young lady named Gale
Who swung from the pub's curtain rail.
When they said, "You are strange!"
She said, "In yonder old grange,
We all swing and drink strong ale!"

## Gale the Blackmailer

There was a young lady named Gale
Who made all her money through blackmail.
When she blackmailed Lee
While out at sea,
It ended in a large killer whale...

## Guy Who Works in AI

I met a young man named Guy
Who works in the field of AI.
His programme writes verse
Which grows steadily worse.
But some say it's written by Guy!

## Holly Who Often Leads Me into Folly

A young lady named Holly
Often leads me into folly.
At just gone midnight,
We met Miss White
And stole her shopping trolley!

# Kate's Improper Date

There was a young lady named Kate
Who went on a most improper date.
The vicar was there
With his mistress Claire
And a waitress who just couldn't wait...!

## Mark Who Is Extremely Fond of the Park

I know a young man named Mark
Who is extremely fond of the park,
Where Claire and Miss Rose
Remove all of their clothes.
Or so I am told by Mark...!

## Poetical Sue

When a poetical young lady named Sue
Wrote an erotic poem about Miss Lou,
A man called Ted
Fell out of bed,
Which left more room for those two...!

# The Affair That Almost Was

When a young lady named Flair
Said, "Would you like an affair?"
I said, "I'm full of anticipation.
But it's busy in Paddington station.
And it might upset the bear!"

# When I Went to a Swingers' Party

When I went to a swingers' party
With my friend who is very arty,
Pretty Miss Ling
Painted a swing
And my friend she painted that party!

## Vicar Ray

When my friend the good vicar Ray
Knelt and said, "Let us all pray."
Sinful Miss Coral
Did something immoral.
And the ambassador urged diplomacy on Ray!

# A Daring Young Lady from South Ealing

A daring young lady from South Ealing
Likes to hang from my bedroom ceiling.
I say to her, "Claire,
We must stop this affair
Or you'll bring down my bedroom ceiling!"

## A Most Philosophical Young Lady Named Page

A most philosophical young lady named Miss Page
Said, "This world is but an unreal stage.
But, let us two dance
And perchance find some romance."
So we did... and crashed through the stage!

## Holly

A most wicked young man named Ted
Said, "I'll put holly in your bed!"
I said, "I strongly object!
You should show some respect."
But Holly was real wicked like Ted!

## A Poet Who Sat Drinking His Wine

A poet who sat drinking his wine
Said, "Young ladies they are truly divine.
But too few women
Are tempted by sinning".
And he wept whilst drinking his wine.

# A Respectable Girl

I know a young lady named Pearl
Who is admired as a respectable girl.
When we meet,
She's always discreet.
So she's admired as a respectable girl...

## A Talented Young Man Riding a Goat

A talented young man riding a goat
Said, "Many a poem I have wrote
About young ladies from Ealing
Who dance on my ceiling.
And can someone please stop this goat!"

# A Young Lady of an Ancient Profession

A young lady of an ancient profession
Has made many a most interesting confession.
She was born into farming
And is really quite charming.
And farming is a very ancient profession...

## A Young Lady Up on a Cloud

A young lady up on a cloud
Said, "Sir, you are speaking too loud!"
I said to her, "Flow,
If I speak too low
You won't hear me on that cloud!"

## A Young Lady Wearing a Very Tight Dress

A young lady wearing a very tight dress
Said, "I have so many sins to confess!"
Then, with a great sneeze,
She spoke of the bees.
And burst out of that very tight dress!

## A Young Lady Who Dresses in Green

A young lady who dresses in green
Is well known on the swinging scene.
My girlfriend Miss Coral
Is really quite moral
And she looks real pretty in green...!

## A Young Lady with Plenty of Money

A young lady with plenty of money
Calls me her sweet and her honey.
Her name, it is Jane
And she's so very plain.
But, dear reader, she's loaded with money...!

## An Interesting Confession

When a young lady made an interesting confession
About her work in the world's oldest profession,
I said, "Working in farming
That is really most charming!"
I am known for my tact and discretion…!

# A Young Man Driving a Large Hearse

A young man driving a large hearse
Said, "This verse is unfinished and terse."

# Fast

As I boarded a brand new train
I met with a girl named Jane.
We went real fast
Then, at long last,
The driver decided to start that train!

# As I Entered My Fine Old Bedroom

As I entered my fine old bedroom,
I met a young lady named Moon.
I said, "My dear,
What brings you here?"
She said, "You're smoking a magic mushroom!"

## As I Strolled Through the Great Crystal Palace

As I strolled through the great Crystal Palace,
I was accosted by that wicked Miss Alice.
After dancing and wine
We crossed that line—
Now I'm missing both my wallet and Alice...

## Seals and Heels

As I swam with my friends the seals,
I met a young lady in stiletto heels
Who said, "To swim
Is surely no sin;
But it's not easy when wearing these heels!"

## One Dark Halloween

As I walked home one dark Halloween
I met a young lady in green.
Her name it was Grace
And back at her place
Sat the devil eating strawberries and cream!

# Hollow

As I walked in a beautiful hollow,
A young lady asked me to follow.
She was pretty and witty
And came from the city.
But, alas, she was so very hollow!

## As I Walked Through the Churchyard Real Late

As I walked through the churchyard real late
I met a young lady named Miss Kate.
When she rattled her chains
And showed me her brains.
I said, "Stop that great racket, Miss Kate!"

## Bess and Her Short Dress

There was a young lady named Bess
Who was known for her short dress.
All the clerics passing by
Would give her the eye.
Then rush off, their sins to confess!

## Beth Who Was Bored to Death

When a young lady whose name is Beth
Said, "you have bored me quite to death!"
I said, with a sigh,
"All flesh it must die.
But sadly Beth you are still drawing breath!"

## Boring Miss Lou

My girlfriend the boring Miss Lou
Is fond of the number 2.
That fascinating Miss Leigh
Is up for 3.
But me I'm stuck with Lou!

## Careless Janine

When a careless young lady named Janine
Slipped and fell into a deep ravine,
She got covered in custard
And some rather nice mustard.
It really was a very strange scene!

## Crushing Old Bore

When a young lady named Moore
Called me a crushing old bore
And I asked her why,
She heaved a great sigh
And then I heard Moore snore!

## The Meaning of Poetry

When a young lady whose name is Fay
Said, "Tell me what your poems do say!"
I said, "Come you near, my dear,
And let me whisper in your ear.
Sweet Fay, they mean what they do say!"

## The Vicarage Lawn

There was a young lady named Dawn
Who made love on the vicarage lawn.
A passing parishioner
Applied lawn conditioner,
Which disconcerted the poor vicar and Dawn!

## Feisty

A young man named Guy
Liked to make women cry.
But pretty Miss Pearl,
Being a feisty girl,
Poked Guy in the eye!

# Fine Art

A young lady named Miss Heart
Is a connoisseur of fine art.
Whilst enjoying some wine,
She greatly admired mine.
And then we discussed fine art.

## Forgetful Miss Brown

A most forgetful young lady named Miss Brown
Is in the habit of losing her gown.
My friend, vicar Glynn,
Says, "We all sin",
As he returns that gown to Miss Brown...

# Grace

I know a young lady named Grace
Who is known for her pretty face.
A girl called Nell
Runs a seedy hotel.
But at least it's graced by Grace!

## Miss Mar's Memoir

My friend whose name is Miss Mar
Wrote a memoir just wearing her bra.
When I attended her book signing,
All the men they where lining
Up to see her memoir and bra...

## Miss Wood and the Mud

When a careless young lady named Wood
Got her stilettos stuck in deep mud
And I said, "Get them off",
She replied, with a shocked cough,
"Not here! In this nasty deep mud!"

## My Posh Girlfriend

My girlfriend, who is so very posh,
Is fond of saying 'golly!' and 'gosh!'
When she's in the mood
She turns wicked and lewd
And you wouldn't believe that she's posh!

## Dating a Vampire

I'm dating a pretty vampire named Wood
Who is rather fond of men's blood.
But she also likes wine,
Which suits me real fine:
As I'm rather fond of my blood!

## Henrietta's Erotic Letter

When a naughty young lady named Henrietta
Sent the bishop an extremely erotic letter,
His wife called her loose
And his daughter turned puce.
And the bishop he treasured that letter...

# I Know a Young Lady in Pink

I know a young lady in pink
Who goes by the name of Spink.
She is known in society
For her lack of sobriety.
And I'm also fond of a drink!

## I Once Had a Lover Named Moon

I once had a lover named Moon
Who, on swallowing a very large balloon,
Said, "I have such a thirst
That I fear I shall burst!"
It was over too soon with Moon

# Last Night as I Homeward Went

Last night as I homeward went,
I met a girl from Kent.
When I recited a rhyme
About the concept of time,
She wept and returned to Kent!

## Literary Miss Lou

A literary young lady named Miss Lou,
Being determined that her book break through,
Lobbed it at the window
Of a publisher I know.
And that book it did break threw!

# Moriah's Passion

A gorgeous young lady named Miss Morriah
Has a passion for the old squire.
She wears stiletto heels
And swims with seals.
But some say the squire's a liar!

## The Old Squire

My dear old friend the late squire
Had a passion for young Miss Moriah.
But his wife Claire
Discovered him with her...
Oh, how I miss the old squire!

# I Once Had a One Night Stand

I once had a one-night stand
With a young lady named Miss Bland.
It may have been December.
But I really don't remember
As that girl was so very bland!

## My Stay in a Seedy Hotel

Whilst staying in a seedy old hotel
I was accosted by pretty Miss Bell.
It is no crime
To indulge in rhyme
About Miss Bell in a seedy hotel...

# Pam's Pram

When I saw my dear friend Miss Pam
Pushing new twins in her very large pram,
I remembered all that wine
And said, "Are they mine?"
Have you ever been hit by a pram?

## Philosophical Gwen

When a philosophical young lady named Gwen
Climbed to the top of Big Ben
And a policeman called Lyme
Said, "tell me the time",
"Time has no real existence", said Gwen!

## Sinful Rose

There was a young lady named Rose
Who was fond of wearing no clothes.
The vicar took her in
And lectured her on sin,
As his wife berated him and Rose…

## Swansong

There was an old man named Long
Who wept as he sang his swansong.
They took off their hats
And whacked him with bats.
And so ended that swansong of long!

# The Foolish Libertarian

There once was a foolish old libertarian
Who was imprisoned in a large aquarium.
When he said, "I am free
To swim in this great sea!"
The fish laughed in that large aquarium!

## There Once Was a Policeman Named Warner

There once was a policeman named Warner
Who raided a rather famous old sauna.
He found Miss Hocking
Without shoe or stocking.
And a politician discussing politics with Lorna...

# There Was a Young Lady of Dundee

There was a young lady of Dundee
Who decided to climb a tall tree.
When they said, "Are you high?"
She said, "That I emphatically deny!
There is no pot in this tree."

## There Was a Young Man Named Dunn

There was a young man named Dunn
Who decided to fly to the sun.
But, going off course,
He encountered a horse
Who said, "That just can't be done!"

# Shopping

Whilst out shopping
I see girl's shoes
And lose
Myself in a shocking
Thought, of stilettos bought
By young women who,
At night
Bring delight
With loss of shoe
And stocking.
But I have shopping
Still to do!

# Contact and Social Media

To contact Kevin, please send an email to kmorrispoet@gmail.com.

Website: https://kmorrispoet.com/

Twitter: https://twitter.com/drewdog2060_

Instagram: https://www.instagram.com/kmorrispoet/

Printed in Great Britain
by Amazon

33425403R00086